JOAN RIVERS AND PATRICE LAPPERT

PHILIP RIVERS
PASSION AND PURPOSE

SOPHIA INSTITUTE PRESS
Manchester, NH

Sophia Institute Press
Box 5284, Manchester, NH 03108
1-800-888-9344

www.SophiaInstitute.com

Sophia Institute Press® is a registered trademark of Sophia Institute.

Library of Congress Control Number:2019946899
First printing

INSIDE

01 Foreword

03 A Boy with Big Dreams

09 Coach's Kid at Athens High

13 College Ball and Comebacks

17 Picking Up Speed with the Chargers

21 Humble Fumble: Finding Success in Failure

27 Friends Off the Field

31 Injuries and Intercessions

39 A Leader on the Field and in the Home

43 Epilogue: Teammates in Holiness

FOREWORD

Philip Rivers is an eight-time NFL Pro Bowl quarterback. He has been with the San Diego Chargers (now the Los Angeles Chargers) since he was drafted in 2004. He is the Chargers' all-time passing leader.

As his mother, I can tell you this: Philip has shown extraordinary passion since the day he was born. Whether it was leading a pickup football game in our backyard or serving as an altar boy, Philip pursued everything with passion.

This is a book to encourage you to pursue your goals, and live your faith, *with passion*.

A BOY WITH BIG DREAMS

Philip Rivers was not always a famous athlete. He was once a kid like you, with big dreams and an even bigger love of sports that started when he was very young. As a toddler, he loved going to Decatur High football games with his father, Steve, who was Decatur's head coach. As the players and coaches worked to become better and better as a team, Philip eagerly and intently watched, hoping to one day be doing the same. Philip practiced everything he learned from those Friday night games. He learned to handle regulation-size footballs, which were heavy for a young boy. To manage the weight, he threw the ball in an unusual sideways motion. He still uses this unique throw as an NFL player today.

The first games Philip led were in our backyard or on the street in front of our house. He would get his friends together for pickup games. Sometimes he would ask Steve or me to announce his name as he ran out onto the field, as in the big leagues.

Even when Philip played by himself, he would imagine he was in front of a huge audience, under the bright lights of an NFL stadium. The clock would be running. He would be searching for an opening, trying to make a game-winning pass. The crowd would be cheering him on. And then — he'd throw the ball down the field for a touchdown!

He hoped that one day his dream would come true.

As he grew up, Philip held on to his dream of playing in the NFL. In fifth grade, his teacher asked the class to make a poster showing what they wanted to be when they grew up. Philip knew exactly what to put on his poster. He cut out a picture of Minnesota Vikings player Anthony Carter that had appeared on the cover of *Sports Illustrated*. Then he glued a picture of his face over Carter's and put the new cutout on his poster.

Steve and I framed Philip's poster, and to this day, more than twenty years later, it remains in our home in Alabama. When Philip visits, he looks at the poster and shakes his head in amazement. How could he have been so fortunate? Many talented football players do not reach the NFL. What made Philip one of the special few who did make it?

Philip would not say his success was all luck. He worked very hard, not just in high school and college, but even as a little boy running along the sidelines, trying to get a glimpse of the determination and skill of the players. Philip understood that he had unique talents and longed for the day that he could participate in the game he loved.

There was something else, too, something you can't always see on TV — something less dramatic than bright lights and big crowds, yet even more awe-inspiring. God had a plan for Philip's life, and Philip knew it. Not just a plan to get him closer to the NFL but to draw him closer to Himself. That is God's plan for all of us.

COACH'S KID AT ATHENS HIGH

The next big step for Philip was varsity football. He joined the Athens High School Golden Eagles in 1996. His head coach was his father, Steve. At first, Philip didn't know if he should call Steve "Dad" or "Coach." Steve said, "Call me Dad." On and off the field, Steve's role as a father came first.

Steve had many tough choices to make as a coach. He knew Philip was a talented quarterback. He wanted to give his son the chance to practice his skills, but the team already had a senior quarterback. Steve decided to have Philip play linebacker that year. Philip didn't complain or question his father. Instead, he worked hard in his new position and became an excellent linebacker and a much tougher football player.

He was a "team first" player. At no time was this more evident than when, as a senior quarterback, several college coaches attended one of his playoff games. The team was having success running the ball when Steve asked Philip, "Do you think we should pass it?" Steve wanted Philip to have a chance to show off his arm for the college coaches.

Philip replied, "No, Dad! Why should we? We are killing them with the running game." Philip valued the entire team's success above his own. He wanted the team to win, even if he had to forgo his chance to stand out.

Sadly, a few games later, the Golden Eagles lost in the third round of the state playoffs. The season was over, most of the team had left, and Philip and his dad sat alone in the locker room. While he was dealing with his disappointment, Philip turned to Steve and said, "I love you, Dad." The painful loss hadn't changed the love between father and son.

This is the kind of love that God, our heavenly Father, offers us. No matter what happens, we can always turn to Him in prayer and say, "I love You." A loving father will always respond with care for his children. Philip trusted in this love as he moved on to the excitement and challenges of college and then professional football.

COLLEGE BALL AND COMEBACKS

Philip joined the North Carolina State Wolfpack in 2000. He was barely eighteen years old. In his new city, he was homesick. The first Sunday, he entered a church for Sunday Mass. He breathed a sigh of relief. He felt at home. To this day, Philip does not miss Mass, no matter what city he is playing in. He realizes that the Church is always his home.

As a freshman college quarterback, Philip noticed that the big difference from high school to college was the speed of the game. He studied the game and learned how to quickly read defenses.

Before long, Philip found his place on his new team. He was named North Carolina State's starting quarterback and quickly proved himself as one of the most gifted players of that time.

Under Philip's leadership, the Wolfpack became known for their comeback victories. The team would rally in the fourth quarter and often score with only seconds left in the game.

After one of these surprise wins Philip's dad said, "As a coach, you never give up on your team, and as a dad, you never give up on your son." Nor does God ever give up on us, His children. When we feel as if we can't succeed and must quit, we can remember these words from the Gospel: "Nothing will be impossible for God" (Luke 1:37). We can make our own surprise comebacks in life, if only we have faith.

PICKING UP SPEED WITH THE CHARGERS

After his stellar college career with fifty-three straight games as a starter, Philip had to wait his turn to start in the NFL. He was drafted by the Chargers in 2004, but for two years he had to serve as backup behind Drew Brees. Although Philip had been drafted to take Brees's place, Brees began enjoying unexpected success. So Philip found himself on the bench as the Chargers' second-string quarterback.

Because of the circumstances, the two teammates could have been bitter rivals. Instead, they became friends and learned from each other. Because they didn't resent each other, both players were able to help each other improve.

In 2006, when Brees signed with the New Orleans Saints, Philip was ready to step in as the Chargers' new starting quarterback. In his first year as starter for the Chargers, he led his team to a stunning 14-2 record. Thus began Philip's rise to becoming one of the NFL's best quarterbacks of all time.

HUMBLE FUMBLE: FINDING SUCCESS IN FAILURE

Even as a professional football player, Philip sometimes made mistakes. During the closing minutes of a game against the Kansas City Chiefs in 2011, Philip experienced one of the most humiliating moments of his career. He mishandled a routine snap from his long-time teammate, center Nick Hardwick, and fumbled the ball. The successful exchange between a professional quarterback and his center is expected in the NFL. For Philip and Nick, it had always been as effortless as a handshake. Philip had just led his team to a game-tying drive in the fourth quarter. Now he was leading another drive that could have won the game. The clock was ticking, and the Chargers were just fifteen yards from scoring. A chip-shot kick would have been enough to win the divisional game and put them on top in the AFC West. Instead, the fumble resulted in a turnover and a shattering loss for the Chargers and for Philip.

He was an elite quarterback playing under the lights in an NFL stadium for an audience of millions, and yet he messed up!

You can imagine how Philip felt. He had no explanation for how he could have mishandled the ball. As a result, he lost his confidence and began worrying all the time that it would happen again. He not only lost his confidence; he lost his peace.

There was only one thing Philip could do with all that pain. He turned to

God. He prayed harder and longer than ever before. Soon, Philip began to feel God's comforting presence. Using prayer books and Bible verses recommended by a holy priest, Philip came to realize that anxiety and worry were not from God. So he let go of his dismay over the fumble, and his confidence was slowly restored. Philip learned to trust in God completely.

Nunc Coepi: Philip's New Motto

Through God's grace, one of the worst moments in Philip's career became one of the greatest moments in his spiritual life. Philip learned many lessons from his "humble fumble." To remind himself of these lessons, Philip adopted a personal motto: *nunc coepi*. In Latin, *nunc coepi* means, "Now we begin." As Philip explains, "In our prayers, in our habits, in our relationships — *nunc coepi* applies to everything. Whether you got a bad grade or didn't do well on a project, you must begin again. Whether I have a bad play or a good play, a touchdown or an interception, I must begin again."

Philip knows that the sacrament of Reconciliation, or Confession, is the best place to go when you need to begin again. In Confession, God embraces you with His mercy and grace. No matter how many times you've messed up, or how big your mistakes have been, He'll forgive you and provide you with the strength to make a new start.

Nunc coepi!

FRIENDS OFF THE FIELD

While recovering from the embarrassment of his "humble fumble," Philip also relied on some of his friends in the Church. A priest friend suggested spiritual reading to help him find encouragement and reassurance. That same priest listened to him in the sacrament of Confession and imparted the actual grace we all need to move forward.

Other friends gave him advice and companionship. Philip got to know the Dominican Sisters of Mary, Mother of the Eucharist, and to this day his children enjoy participating in the virtue camp that the sisters sponsor each year in San Diego.

The sisters have been important supporters of Philip and the Chargers. They pray that God will watch over the team and help them play well. Like Philip, they enjoy the many ways in which faith and football overlap. They especially love "Hail Mary" passes, those long, desperate throws made in the final seconds of a game to avoid defeat. The name suggests that the passes need Our Lady's help to be completed.

Philip has thrown his fair share of Hail Mary passes during his career. He has also said plenty of Hail Marys before major plays. You may have noticed him praying before each offensive series. In times of need, he trusts that God and the saints will help him, though he doesn't always know how or when this help will come. He understands that God often acts in ways that surprise us. This was the case when He helped Philip through two major injuries.

INJURIES AND INTERCESSIONS

On January 13, 2007, the Chargers were playing the Indianapolis Colts in the AFC divisional playoff game. During the third quarter, Philip suddenly felt a snap in his knee. He fell to the ground and was taken off the field to the locker room.

He was excited when he saw his team defeat the Colts that day. The Chargers were moving on to play in the AFC Championship game against the New England Patriots. The winner of that game would go on to the Super Bowl!

But Philip and the team doctors knew something was wrong. They X-rayed his knee, and the results were not good. Two important ligaments in Philip's knee had been damaged, including his ACL, which was completely torn.

The doctors told Philip he needed surgery, with months of rehab to follow. Philip couldn't believe the news. He asked if there was any way he could play in the championship game, but the doctors told him that would be impossible. Philip was heartbroken.

Then I called him with news that gave him great hope. "Philip," I said excitedly. "We just realized that next Sunday is St. Sebastian's feast day!"

The championship game would be played on the feast day of St. Sebastian, the patron saint of athletes and a special friend of Philip's. Throughout his professional career Philip has brought a St. Sebastian

medal and prayer card to every game. He now believed this was a sign that he'd be able to play in the championship game after all.

That Sunday, Philip prepared himself well. He went to Mass and received the Eucharist. His knee was taped up tight, and he went on to play in the championship — with a torn ACL. The Chargers didn't win the game that day, but Philip played well and found peace. He had won a battle of strength and courage instead, with the help of St. Sebastian.

During the 2014 season, Philip sustained another injury, this time in his back. The injury was so severe that it caused numbness in his leg. When the season was over, the doctors urged Philip to undergo back surgery. But Philip wanted to avoid surgery at all costs.

While on vacation in Florida, Philip went to Sunday Mass. He prayed fervently about whether he should have the surgery. As he was leaving the church, he heard someone call out, "Philip! How's your back?"

Surprised that this stranger would know about his injury, Philip answered, "It's okay, I guess." While football players are often recognized in public, Philip was two-thousand miles from home, and he hadn't spoken much in public about his back injury.

The man replied, "I can help your back injury." Philip couldn't believe what he was hearing. He was even more amazed when the man, a physical therapist, introduced himself as Bob Seton, because Philip and his wife, Tiffany had recently chosen St. Elizabeth Ann Seton as the patron saint of their family and their home school. This may seem like a coincidence, but God has a way of communicating answered prayers to those who pray faithfully. Once again, a dear heavenly friend, this time St. Elizabeth Ann Seton, had stepped in to help Philip in his time of need. God had answered his prayers. Bob Seton was able to give Philip the therapy he needed so that surgery was no longer necessary.

The help of St. Sebastian and St. Elizabeth Ann Seton inspired Philip to see the Church as one big team. Our heavenly teammates — the saints — intercede for us, which means they take our prayers directly to God, who is present to them in Heaven in a much closer way than He is to us on Earth. Like each member of a football team, the saints all have special roles. There's a patron saint for almost anything you can imagine!

A LEADER ON THE FIELD AND IN THE HOME

St. Elizabeth Ann Seton has been a wonderful patron of Philip's family, watching over Philip, Tiffany, and their children. Philip's family is a very important part of his life. He and his wife were middle school sweethearts, and they decided to get married when Philip was still in college. Their first child was born fifteen months later. Now they have nine children, two boys and seven girls.

Philip's commute between San Diego and Los Angeles takes about ninety minutes, but he still gets home in time for dinner. He listens to his children talk about their day, and then he tucks them in at night.

Few moments in Philip's life are as precious as those he spends with his family. His home can be a busy place with so many children, but Philip knows that each child is a gift from God. As Mother Teresa said, "Children are like flowers: you can never have too many of them."

Football players enjoy a great deal of fame. Wealth and status can be strong sources of temptation, but Philip hasn't let them distract him from his role as a husband and father. He even turned down his chance to play in the Pro Bowl in 2010 so he wouldn't miss the birth of his fifth child.

Philip's family helps him remain down-to-earth. Changing diapers and meeting the daily challenges of a big family keep him focused on what's really important. Being the leader of the team we call "family," and leading this team to the victory of Heaven, is his most important role.

EPILOGUE: TEAMMATES IN HOLINESS

Philip Rivers has made a long journey from playing pickup games in our backyard to leading an NFL team. The young boy who dreamed of gridiron success is now an eight-time Pro Bowl quarterback and the Chargers' all-time passing leader. You can find his name on many lists of top-ranked football players. Young NFL hopefuls can now cut out *his* picture and add it to their own school projects.

Philip's journey hasn't always been easy. He has won some big games and lost some big games. He has had injuries and made mistakes. In good times and in bad, he has relied on the graces that God provides us through the Catholic Church. As a loving Father, God has taken care of Philip and his family. He watches over them — just as He watches over you. He has plans for your life, even if you don't know what they are yet. If you lose your way, you can always turn to God and ask Him to help you "begin again," just as Philip does.

Always remember that you and Philip are part of the same special team: the Church. Your faith joins you and Philip together in Christ. As teammates, you're working toward the same goal of growing in holiness. God gave Philip a unique way of serving Him as a football player. God has given you, too, your own special gifts to develop so that you can live a holy life. May Philip's example strengthen your faith and give you courage as you continue your journey to Heaven — the greatest journey of all. *Nunc coepi.*